HISTORY OF STEAM

ON THE

ERIE CANAL.

Appeal for the Extension of the Act of April, 1871, "to Foster and Develop the Inland Commerce of the State,"

FOR THE BENEFIT OF THE CANALS

AND THE

COMMERCIAL COMMUNITY.

NEW YORK, JANUARY, 1873.

NEW YORK:

EVENING POST STEAM PRESSES, 41 NASSAU STREET, COR. LIBERTY.

1873.

With Respects of the Author,

155 *Broadway, N. Y.*

HISTORY OF STEAM

ON THE

ERIE CANAL.

Screw Propellers from 1858 to 1862.

During the maple sugar season of the spring of 1858, a well-to-do farmer, of western New York, whittled out a spiral or augur-like screw-propeller, in miniature, which he thought admirably adapted to the canal. He soon after went to Buffalo, and contracted for a boat to be built, with two of his Archimedean screws for propulsion by steam.

Although advised by his builders to substitute the common four-bladed propellers, he adhered to his original design, and with one propeller at either side of the rudder—called "twin-propellers"—she was soon ready for duty. She is the vessel known to history as the *Charles Wack.*

She carried three-fourths cargo and towed another boat with full cargo, and made the trip from Buffalo to West Troy in seven days, total time, averaging two miles per hour. But she returned from Troy to Buffalo, with half freight, in four days and sixteen hours, net time; averaging three and one-twelfth miles per hour, without tow.

This initiated the series of steamers from 1858 to 1862, and, with others that soon followed, created a general enthusiasm in behalf of steam transportation, which led to a trip through the canal that fall, on a chartered steam-tug, by the Governor of the State, the Canal Board, and other notables, and with public receptions, speeches, &c., at different cities along the route.

That boat was soon followed by the *S. B. Ruggles*, a first-class steam canal-boat, built by the Hon. E. S. Prosser, of Buffalo, with a first-class modern propeller, and with double the engine capacity of the former.

The *P. L. Sternburg* soon followed, and was a first-class boat, with modern twin-propellers, but with less engine capacity than the *Wack*.

The same season there were some local steamers built to run regularly between different cities on the line of the canal.

The following season of 1859 was the most active year the Erie Canal has ever known in regard to steam.

The *C. Wack* was sold to Mr. Prosser, who took out her Archimedean propellers, and substituted a modern propeller, and doubled her engine capacity, and reproduced her as the *City of Buffalo*.

The *Gold Hunter* was produced by the Western Transportation Company, of Buffalo. She was a short, oblong tub, with a square, box-like bow, and rounded stern, designed only to carry machinery and coal, and was to be recessed into the stern of ordinary horse-boats by cutting away an equivalent space therefrom. She was designed to make a trip on the canal, and be immediately transferred to another boat for return trip, thus to avoid the usual loss of time at the termini of the canal. She was abandoned after a brief trial.

The canal-boat *Niagara* had the Cathcart propeller supplied, which consisted of a union of the propeller and rudder by a universal joint in the shaft, and so adjusted as to unite them for steerage purposes. This design was tried on the steamer *Cathcart*, upon the Chesapeake and Ohio Canal, in 1858, and with considerable newspaper *eclat*.

The *Rotary*, of New York, was a new steamer for freighting purposes, with a rotary engine and common propeller. This occupied but little space, and worked prettily on exhibition.

The *Eclipse*, of New York, was new, and had oscillating propeller engines.

Screw-Tugs.

The *Gov. King* was a medium-sized New York harbor propeller, and made repeated trips with three boats in tow, and one trip with five boats. She was so slow as to be unremunerative, as compared with horses.

The Western Transportation Co., after the failure of the *Gold Hunter*, built two powerful tugs, the *Washington* and *Lafayette*. They were soon withdrawn.

Mr. Prosser built the first-class tug, *Stimers*, but she had a short canal history.

The tugs, *Bemis* and *Dan Brown*, made good runs each, with three boats in tow, but were short-lived canallers.

Paddle-wheels and other Devices.

During these years the paddle-wheel system was thoroughly tried, and under varied circumstances.

As the locks prevented the use of side-wheels for full freights, an adjustable stern-wheel was tried. This could be raised or lowered in adaptation to the light or full cargo.

The *H. K. Viele* was a first-class canal steamer, with stern-wheel and vertical, or excentric, acting paddles. These were considered by some as peculiarly well adapted to canal purposes, yet in practice proved otherwise.

The *Fall Brook* was built by Mr. John McGee, of Seneca Lake renown, for towing purposes, intending to establish a line between Seneca Lake and New York city ; but her canal abilities were so poor as to cause her withdrawal to lake duty.

She had powerful engines, with vertical acting paddle-wheel, set amidships between twin-hulls, with a full flow of water from bow to stern, and was decked across forward and aft of her wheel.

The *Lady Jane*, of Utica, was a bow paddle-wheel boat with small engines. She accomplished but little.

As paddle-wheel canallers have proven less efficient than screw propellers they are more limited in numbers.

Other contemporary devices were tried.

The canal-boat, *Oswego*, had her stern recessed to receive a submerged horizontal, centrifugal-acting water-wheel, which received water at a central and ejected it at a periphery opening for propulsion.

This opening could be turned for steerage or backing purposes. She was altered at Green Point and received good machinery at Brooklyn, but was soon restored to horses.

Duck's-feet paddles were experimented with at Buffalo. A scull propulsion was tried upon the Hudson. Also hinge-bladed propellers, to open and close with a fore-and-aft movement at the stern. This last device was tried by a Doctor Hunter, who has more recently tried a "Fish-Tail Propeller," the blades being made of rubber, to imitate the form and elasticity of the tail, with mechanical imitations of movement.

It is hardly necessary to add that these devices were all worthless, and others of miscellaneous character may have been tried, yet without merit.

Remarks.

Wealth, experience and skill have marked this first era of steam, and though combined, they utterly failed. Both Mr. Prosser and the Western Transportation Co. were owners of fleets of splendid lake propellers, and were wealthy, with interests intimately identified with canals. It is evident there was no want, either of money, mechanical resources, or knowledge of canal business as basis of their failures with steam.

Capital flowed into the steam enterprise from various resources, and ambition multiplied experiments, but with no appreciable success.

The difficulties lay beyond the reach of capital and beyond the reach of known resources, and no adequate knowledge had been developed to solve the problem. Therefore, after suffering failures for several years, the State wisely volunteered to add extraordinary inducements by a large appropriation to encourage SUCCESS. It could not have been to encourage the reproduction of former failures by the repetition of former trials.

The inquiry is therefore proper, as a lesson from the history of the early era of steam, what are the difficulties? Why has steam failed so absolutely and so universally? Why did the State subsequently offer a large bounty to foster and develop steam.

Obviously there is some hidden difficulty, some unknown inability, because steam is the arbiter of the age, it is the great supreme motor of man's agencies throughout the world, hence we come from the sublime to the ridiculous when we use it to load boats at Buffalo, to be towed 350 miles by horses.

The lessons of the early era are worthless for repetition. There is no better screw-propelling machinery known than was then tried and abandoned; but the lessons are of value to discover the difficulties which must be remedied; to teach that the success of steam lies beyond the reach of publicly known mechanical resources.

The trials establish plainly and incontrovertibly that the failures were owing to the want of *mechanical adaptation* to required duty; to a *mechanical inability* to utilize the power of the steam; to a *mechanical waste* of power beyond their ability to control or remedy; and that the wasted power was extravagantly large and the utilized insignificantly small. A very intelligent captain of one of the best and most powerful steamers known to the Erie Canal, who had a full and carefully-kept log, stated that when his engine *exceeded* a hundred horse-power of steam, he could only equal twelve horses on the tow-path. Thus over seven-eighths of his power was wastefully developed in order to render one-eighth useful. But this occurred when he was moving only two loaded boats—the steamer and one in tow—but when moving four boats—three in tow—the *percentage of utility* was lessened, and he could not exceed eight to ten per cent. of his steam, as shown in slower movement, when fewer horses on the tow-path could equal him.

The steamer is a reservoir, and its rotatory power is free to be developed "*inversely as its resistances.*" Hence, when fastened to a pier, it is all developed in its receding currents, and *per contra* when moving; if its machinery had a perfect fulcrum, it would all be developed in the run of the boat; consequently, on rivers and lakes, with fine-lined steamers, that cut the water like a knife, it is like standing in a small boat and pushing from a large one, but on canals, with their full bows, it is like standing in a large boat and pushing from a small one; the little one runs away with the power. The more than 100 square feet area of immersed section of the full bow represents the large boat, and the dozen square feet effective area of propeller blades, set at an easy angle for spiral motion and recession velocity, is the little one that squanders the power so extravagantly. Increase in number of boats increases this contrast. The propeller blades of a good canaller will move twelve to fifteen miles, in their line of spiral movement, to get two to three miles headway for the boat.

A correct scientific analysis can trace the developments of the eighty-five to ninety per cent. of the inherent power of the steam that is wasted on the common canal-boat, and that has no resultant effect whatever in the motion of the boat, just as positively as it can trace the co-developments of fifteen to ten per cent. that is utilized and that moves the boat.

The practical man sees the truths of these statements. He sees steam used with small, medium and large engines for canal purposes, and sees them all fail to meet the economy of transportation established by horses; but he would just as soon put men on the tow-path to compete with horses as to put horses into his elevators to compete with steam; and that, because in the elevators the power of the steam is chiefly utilized, whilst on the canal it is chiefly wasted.

It is therefore conclusive that there is an absolute necessity for a NEW MECHANICAL SYSTEM, for a radically different system of transmissive mechanism, for a system that can develop a considerable portion of the power of the steam in the movement of boats.

The variations of the old systems of propulsion that are being continuously tried are worthless, in the very nature of the case, because they are in no sense a remedy for existing inabilities, and because they do not, in any sense whatever, meet the difficulties.

STEAM IN 1871 AND 1872.

Screw Propellers.

Soon after the Act of April, 1871, to foster and develop the inland commerce of the State, the steam canal-boat *Cathcart* was tried. She is like the *Niagara* of 1859, and has not been continued in the trade.

The canal-boat *George Barnard*, afterward called the *Andrew H. Dawson*, was tried, and has run through the season of 1872. She has a common propeller in her bow, with a recess from the water-line inclined to twenty feet aft to the bottom. Her propeller, therefore, forces the current against this incline and along the bottom in retardation of its progress. Hence, she cannot be expected to excel former trials.

The *Eureka* is an iron boat, built at Buffalo, with twin-propellers at her bow, set in recesses, at a diverging angle, to throw the water from the bow along the sides of the boat. She is built, by men of canal experience, with compound engines, and was designed to be a superior boat for canal purposes. But her *mechanical currents* at and against the bow must have a retarding tendency, not compensated by any other considerations.

The *George A. Feeter* is also a twin-propeller, with diagonal, channel waterways on each side for about twenty-five feet, when they merge into a larger channel about five feet forward of the rudder. Her propellers are set in these channels, about ten feet aft of their side openings. With her propellers thus housed, the mechanical currents against the aft-sides of her channels are very damaging to her efficiency.

The *Wm. Baxter* is also a twin propeller, like the *P. L. Sternburg*, of 1858, and with compound engines, like the *Eureka* and the *Dawson.* She is built of yellow pine, with easy lines, and so low as to be unable to carry five-sixths of a horse-cargo of wheat or corn below deck, so that her lightness gives help to cargo, and her sharp bow and stern to speed. But her construction and model were long since abandoned by canal-boat builders.

The *Wm. Newman* is a common propeller and double-deck boat, and carries two hundred and ten tons. She is much like the *Ruggles* of 1858, but has less steam capabilities.

The *Charles Hemjee* was built upon the Western Division, with a tunnel-shaped encasement to her propeller. Of course she is reported as "very slow."

The *John Durston* had a propeller built in with her rudder, and driven with a vertical shaft, extending down through a cylindrical rudder-post, but was unfit for service.

Paddle Wheels.

The *Port Byron* is a stern, paddle-wheel boat, with vertical or eccentric acting paddles, and is like the *Viele* of 1858. She has a recess the entire length of her bottom of several square feet area, intended to facilitate a flow of water from the bow, but the flow does not occur; the mechanical currents of the wheel will be from the nearest water, and not from ninety feet forward.

The *Montana* is a similar stern-wheeler, without the recess.

The *Success* consists of two sections, to be disconnected for passing the locks, with paddle-wheel machinery at the bow. Her wheel, inside of the paddles, is a drum or cylinder, filled with cork, to be buoyant, and the hull has an easy, scow bow, for the water to pass under the boat. Practically, the large drum makes her a horizontal, cylindrical-bowed boat, and she mechanically throws the water therefrom against the scow-shaped bow, and so that the cylinder displacement with the mechanical currents, and the scow-bow displacement, combine to make her *very slow.* With her two sections she brought one and a half cargoes of corn.

The *Excelsior* has a horizontal, eccentric-acting paddle wheel, and was built of light iron at Green Point. She had a recess at the bow for her submerged wheel, and, when thus tried, found the retarding effects of the mechanical currents at and against the bow so great, as to cause her original bow-propulsion to be made stern-propulsion, when she was much improved. She was tried with cargo for a short distance on the canal, and withdrawn.

The *Fountain City* is a common boat, with machinery at her stern. She has two submerged horizontal, excentric-acting paddle-wheels, each of small diameter. These are placed under her quarters, in the rudder cross-section, and she is steered by her machinery. The characteristics of these wheels are like the *Excelsior's*, and the excentric variations of both—together with the *Byron's*, *Montana's* and *Viele's*—are known as old devices of secondary merit on river, lake and ocean steamers.

The *Santiago* is a scow-boat, with a recess, or flume, the whole length of her bottom, to a stern propeller. Her steam was soon abandoned.

An endless-chain propulsion was tried upon the Western Division, without success.

A common canal-boat has been experimented with at Brooklyn to propel her by the reaction of a powerful blower or fan. This was driven first by a ten-horse, and next by a forty-horse stationary engine, and afterwards by a forty-horse oscillator. Each failed to move her from her slip, and the conception proved an absurdity.

In addition to these, local steamers have been run between different cities for local purposes, more or less, since 1858, and steam-tugs have been brought into requisition occasionally.

OBSERVE:

This review presents the important fact, that NO NEW MECHANICAL SYSTEM HAS BEEN INTRODUCED.

The screw-propellers and paddle-wheels are multiplications from the former era. The variations from the common propeller and paddle-wheel, in the miscellaneous devices, are all under *reductions of merit.*

All the bow-propulsions, and all the variations from the *Viele*, *Sternburg* and *Ruggles* of the former, and the *Byron*, *Baxter* and *Newman* of the present era, are inferior, whether viewed practically or scientifically.

Hence, steam has received no mechanical advancements since 1858; and the efforts of 1872 are as positive and determinate failures as those of 1862.

THE TRIALS OF STEAM IN 1872 LESS ECONOMICAL THAN IN 1858 TO 1862.

It should be observed that the first trials of steam in 1858 were made during a season of low water, and when the Canal Board had limited the loading of boats to four and three-fourths feet draught of water, which, later in the season, was increased to five feet, and in subsequent years to six feet, as continued to the present time.

Among the most successful trials of the first era of steam on the canals, may be mentioned the *H. K. Viele*, *P. L. Sternburg*, and *S. B. Ruggles.* Each could carry three-fourths cargo and tow a full cargo, and each exceed the speed of horse-boats.

Among the most successful trials of the present era may be mentioned the *Port Byron, Baxter*, and *Newman.* Each can carry five-sixths of a common cargo, and exceed the speed of horses.

In the early era of steam, *the prominent policy* was to combine towage with carrying capacity by the steamer, for economical expedition. In the present era, it has been to make the carrying capacity of the steamer, in itself, economical and expeditious.

This latter policy has arisen under the Appropriation Act of April, 1871, which limits the minimum cargo to two hundred tons, and the minimum average speed of three miles per hour. But these limitations must cover a superior economy of freight transportation to that by the former trials with steam. Else, they are worthless; else, they are failures, as in 1862, and their general introduction impracticable.

As in the steamers *Byron, Baxter* and *Newman, there is nothing mechanically new*, in variation from the *Viele, Sternburg* and *Ruggles*—these trios being *respectively mechanical counterparts of each other;* the paddle-wheels of the *Byron and Viele*, the twin-propellers of the *Baxter* and *Sternburg*, and the common propellers of the *Newman* and *Ruggles*, being respectively identical—the economical features are easily considered.

The first trio can carry 200 tons at good speed; the second can carry 180 tons, and tow 240 tons; total, 420 tons, at good speed.

To the first trio, two boats of each class must be altered; two sets of machinery must be furnished; two corps of engineers maintained, and coal for two round trips must be supplied, with incidental expenses to two steamers, to move 400 tons of freight.

To the second trio, only one boat of each class is to be altered; one set of machinery furnished; one corps of engineers maintained, and coal for one round trip supplied, with the incidental expenses, to move 420 tons of freight.

The costs of alterations and adaptations of the first trio are two-fold those of the second; the cost of machinery greater to the first trio than to the second; the costs of engineers two-fold to the first trio; the costs of coal about the same to each, with greater incidental expenses to the first than to the second *per tons of freight moved.*

The differences in the two trios are in their *steam capabilities and in their times*; the second requires about one day extra on the canal, as possibly due to the locking of the tow, though no extra time is required where both locks of the pair are ready. But the extra twenty tons of freight more than pays the extra time.

The times of transit or rates of speed to the two eras are very nearly alike, the steamers of the first having *greater steam capabilities*, as due to their boat in tow, whilst those of the present era have reduced their steam capabilities to increase their cargoes from the 180 tons to 200 tons.

The times of transit, or rates of speed, are given in the following miscellaneous record, and as published, from time to time, from 1858 to 1862:

The *Wack* was 7 days, total time, with boat in tow, from Buffalo to Troy.

" 4 days 16 hours, net time, with half freight, from Troy to Buffalo.

The *Sternburg* was 28 hours, total time, with boat in tow, from Buffalo to Rochester, 93 miles, averaging 3⅓ miles per hour.

The *Ruggles* was 5½ days, net time, with boat in tow, from Buffalo to Troy, and 6 days 14 hours, net time, from Buffalo to New York.

The *Eclipse* was 7½ days, total time, without tow, from Buffalo to Troy, and 5½ days, total time, without tow, from Troy to Buffalo.

The *Gold Hunter* was 7 days 5 hours, total time, without tow, from Buffalo to Troy.

The *Rotary* was 4 days 4 hours, total time, with half freight, from Troy to Buffalo, and 3 days 16 hours, net time.

The *Bemis*, a screw-tug, with three boats, was 5 days and 8 hours, net time, from Buffalo to Schenectady, 321 miles, average $2\frac{1}{2}$ miles per hour.

The *Washington*, do., with 3 boats, was 5 days 2 hours, net time, from Buffalo to Cohoes, 340 miles, average $2\frac{3}{4}$ miles per hour.

The *Dan Brown*, do., with three boats, was 6 days, net time, from Buffalo to Albany, 351 miles, average nearly $2\frac{1}{2}$ miles per hour; and was 7 hours from Buffalo to Lockport, 31 miles, averaging $4\frac{2}{3}$ miles per hour.

Years 1871 and 1872, as Published.

The *Dawson* and the *Cathcart* have both made and repeated through trips from Buffalo to Troy, with $\frac{5}{8}$ of horse cargoes, in about 7 days, total time.

The *Port Byron* was 5 days $10\frac{1}{2}$ hours, total time, and 4 days 7 hours, net time, with 117 tons of freight, from Troy to Buffalo, from Oct. 29th to Nov. 4th. *The more important down time* was not published.

The *Baxter* was 5 days 14 hours, total time, and 4 days 9 hours, net time, with half freight, from Troy to Buffalo, from Oct. 29th, in the morning, to Nov. 3d; from Sept. 30th to Oct. 5th she was 5 days on her up trip, and early in September was 5 days, also, from Troy to Buffalo.

On her first trip down she left Buffalo Sept. 12th, and arrived at West Troy, the 19th, in 7 days 4 hours, total time, and reached New York the 21st, in 8 days 13 hours, total time, with 200 tons of freight. In some way she reduces her 7 days 4 hours to 4 days 8 hours, net time, to Troy; and her 8 days 13 hours, to New York, to 5 days 17 hours.

Second trip down was from Buffalo to Waterford, when she was longer upon the canal than on her first trip of over 7 days.

Third trip down, left Buffalo Nov. 9th, and arrived at Troy 15th, and New York 17th, or over 6 days to Troy, and 8¼ to New York, with ⅚ horse cargo. This canal trip was during the horse epidemic, and the large number of boats laid up made it very favorable for steam.

But the *Baxter's times* have been developed by a model which would require *one-third of a common boat to be rebuilt*—one-sixth at the bow and one-sixth at the stern—it is, therefore, proper to state, that if we put her machinery and steam capabilities into a common boat—and the seven thousand such boats cannot be dispensed with—it would be *very slow*, as her speed would be reduced by three causes:

1st. Because of an increased velocity of bow displacement at a reduced speed of boat.

2d. Because of an increased velocity of stern replacement, at a reduced speed of boat, against the mechanical or counteracting propelling currents.

3d. Because the percentage of wasted power is increased, and of utilized is diminished, by greater resistance to motion.

The *Wm. Newman* left New York Oct. 30th, and arrived at Buffalo Nov. 7, in 8 days, with 120 tons of freight.

Relations of Time—Twelve Years Ago and Now.

The *Wack's* through time from Buffalo to West Troy, with boat in tow, is the same as the *Baxter's* average without tow.

The *Ruggles'* net time, from Buffalo to New York, with boat in tow, is only 21 hours in excess of the *Baxter's* shortest net time without tow.

The through times of the *Eclipse* and *Gold Huuter*, from Buffalo to West Troy, without tow, are just equal to the *Baxter's* first and second trips.

The *Rotary's* through time up, with half freight, is nearly one day less than the *Byron's*, *Baxter's* or *Newman's* shortest through time. Her net time is 17 hours less than the *Baxter's* shortest net time.

The net time of the tugs, each with three boats in tow, is nearly equal to the *Baxter's* without tow, from Buffalo to West Troy.

Therefore, by this comparison of times, the one day extra allowed for the greater steam resources of the former era with a boat in tow, is ample ; and the policy of that era is plainly more economical for freight than that of the past two years.

We therefore observe: That the policy of introducing steam canal-boats as carriers of freight, is illustrated in the *Niagara*, *Eclipse*, *Gold Hunter* and *Rotary*. The policy of carrying and towing one boat, in the *Wack*, *Sternburg*, *Ruggles*, *City of Buffalo* and *Viele*. The policy of screw-tugs in the *Gov. King*, *Bemis*, *Washington*, *Lafayette*, *Stimers*, *Dan Brown* and the paddle-wheel tug *Fall Brook*. Under each policy steam was a failure on the canals under the agencies tried. The single carriers died first; the tugs second; the carriers and one boat third ; and last, the carriers with three-boat tows.

In 1861 and 1862, the policy of using the powerful canal steamers, *Ruggles* and *City of Buffalo*, to carry freight and tow three boats each, was introduced to supersede the former policies. During these years the privilege of priority at locks, by paying double toll on the boats, was suspended, and soon thereafter steam was totally abandoned.

It is noticeable that the steamers for carrying, only, had less vitality, and were less economical, than those for carrying and towing, and those for carrying and towing but one boat had less than those for carrying and also towing three boats.

Hence, the carrying steamers, or the automaton policy of

1871 and 1872, can only compare with the automaton policy of the former era, and they must have less vitality, and be less economical, than those other for carrying and towing one boat, and still less than those for carrying and towing three boats.

Steam in 1872 Less Economical than Horses.

It has been clearly shown that STEAM in 1872 is less economical than in 1858 to 1860, and still less so than in 1861 and 1862.

But STEAM, in its former history, failed to compete with HORSES; and as, in its recent history, it has failed to be as economical as in its former, because of less economical policies of introduction (machinery being substantially the same), it follows that its failure to compete with horses must be still more marked, still more disappointing to the hopes entertained by the Legislative Department of the State, that independent financial encouragement could possibly foster and develop steam successfully, than it was in its former most significant failures.

But steam in 1872—independent of its failure as compared to itself in 1858—is shown to be less economical than horses by *direct comparison of steamers and horse-boats.*

As steamers have run under a prospective bounty of one hundred thousand dollars for a success, *they have been first-class in all their appointments*, and have been, as in the language of one of their engineers, "rushed through," it is strictly proper to compare them with a well-known duty of *first-class horse-boats*, under the ordinary business enterprise of their captains.

Thus, the first-class modern horse-boat can carry a cargo of 8,800 bushels, or 244 tons of corn, and make seven round trips between New York and Buffalo per season, averaging a round trip per month for the season of navigation.

The most systematic and business-like trials *that have made speed an element of competitive economy*, are the *Port Byron*, *Baxter* and *Newman.*

The short lives of the *Viele* and the *Fall Brook* in canal service, render it unnecessary to give details of the *Byron.*

The *Baxter* left New York late in August or early in September, in new and perfect equipment, in a supposed race for a hundred thousand dollars, and through September, October and to the 19th of November was in the trade, and was in a contest for superiority or supremacy. During this time she delivered at New York two freights, and at Waterford one freight, being the *equivalent* of three freights of 7,200 bushels each, or a total of 21,600 bushels of corn; with runs *equivalent* to two and two-thirds round trips.

But she had priority at locks and right of way at all times, so that the horse-boat, at the sound of her steam whistle, when fifty feet behind, must stop and lay over to the towpath and let her pass. Under these privileges and benefits she was enabled to make her first time between Buffalo and West Troy, as advertised, in a few hours over (7) seven days; her second, required still longer time; her third, being when the horse-disease had nearly " tied up " all other boats, so that she had a river-like freedom, she required about (6) six days, thus *averaging about* (7) seven days from the Lakes to the Hudson.

Give any first-class horse-boat captain a supposed or possible bounty of a hundred thousand dollars, with priority at locks and right of way, and he would in the same time have delivered three times 8,800, or a total of 26,400 bushels of corn from the Lakes to the *Baxter's* destinations; or 4,800 bushels of corn in excess of the *Baxter's* capabilities; and have delivered at Buffalo the same up-freights, with ease.

But the profits of this excess pays a profit over the entire cost of horse-movement, leaving the *Baxter* in debt for her entire cost of movement, for her entire time, and an excess in addition.

Again, suppose *Baxter's* were multiplied and *reduced to horseboat regulations*, then she would have to make eleven trips to deliver at tidewater the freight of nine horse-trips—as $11\times7{,}200=9\times 8{,}800$. This she cannot do in the *same time*, nor can she do it at the *same expense*. Her necessity for the two extra trips would destroy her economy and practicability, or her competitive abilities as against horses.

Hence she is obviously and largely deficient in economy as compared to first-class horse-boat.

The *Wm. Newman* run 5,000 miles from May 17th to November 7th, carrying in the aggregate 2,330 tons of freight. Her time is $5\frac{2}{3}$ months; her mileage is five round trips from Buffalo to and from New York, by the canal 1,000 miles round, each; her freightage is (5×210 or) 1,050 tons down and (5×120 or) *about* 600 tons up, total 1,650 tons This amount carried indicates a towage of two boats down with full freight, and up, through the canal, with half freight; all of which make her aggregate tonnage.

If we allow one and two-thirds months for her towing trip, and leave four months for her four round trips, or a run of 4,000 miles, delivering in New York (4×210 or) 840 tons, and in Buffalo (4×120 or) 480 tons, total 1,320 tons, it may be supposed nearly correct in the absence of details.

A horse-boat, in same time and circumstances, would have made the 4,000 miles and have delivered in New York (4×244 or) 976 tons, and at Buffalo (4×120 or) 480 tons, total 1,456 tons. Excess of down freight 136 tons, equivalent to 4,850 bushels of corn. To make this wantage of freight good, requires nearly two-thirds of a full cargo, or of a full round trip. Hence, she is obviously and largely deficient in economy, as compared to a first-class horse-boat.

Therefore steam in 1872 *is less economical than horses.*

Horse-Boat Times.

Under another view of the case we have the following relations of horses and steam to show that steam in 1872 is less economical than horses.

The captain of the *Vosburg* states that he left West Troy in Oct., carrying over 100 tons of freight, after the *Baxter* had left there for Buffalo, *and with two mule teams,* alternating one with the other every six hours, he arrived at Buffalo in advance of the *Baxter; through time less than the Baxter's shortest time.* "Net time" not stated.

Publishing *net time* of steamers instead of total or through time, is deceptive, and creates a false impression with the community. Had not the through time of steamers this season been suppressed, the governor of the State would not have imagined five-day trips from Buffalo to New York, as per his message, and our city editors would not have ventilated such visionary pretensions. There are a multitude of horse-boat captains that can reduce their *net canal time of movement* below the *Baxter's*, which has been so extensively commented upon; but their so doing would not expedite the transfer of grain from the lakes to tide-water.

A certain horse-boat, in a former season, made two round trips from Buffalo to and from New York in twenty days each, and on each trip lay three days in New York. This made her through time *average* between the cities 8½ days each way. Her captain once towed in the "Line" and was only nine days twenty hours from Buffalo to New York. This season a horse-boat made the round trip from New York to and from Buffalo in twenty-one days.

These *round trips* have probably never been exceeded by steam.

In the former era the prism of the canal seemed imbedded with innumerable old and broken tow-lines, which the propeller, by its high velocity, sucked up, and was thereby "fouled;" and now the sea-grass is a hidden enemy that entwines itself around the propeller to foul it.

When the waters are low, forcing the engines of screw propellers lets the stern of the boat "squat" or hug the bottom, and although these are minor features of want of mechanical adaptation to canal duty, they illustrate petty detentions serving to lengthen the through times of steam.

Hence, if we intermix the slow steamers with the fast ones, as we do the slow with the fast horse-boats, for a *general average*, it is quite probable that horse-times are fully equal to those of steam, and that the excess of horse-cargoes makes a large and handsome advantage in their favor.

Therefore, under this general average, steam in 1872 *is less economical than horses.*

Conditional Explanations.

Because steam has been encouraged by the Legislature, heralded by the press, and favorably reported by the Executive officers of the State as a standard of advancement most desirable to attain, *a supposition very generally prevails outside of canal men that it will succeed.*

As early as 1845, before the enlargements, three steamers were built and tried, and one, the *Pioneer*, ran from New York to Oswego in five days, total time, 362 miles; and *then* "*supposition very generally prevailed that steam would succeed.*" But light freights would not pay then as against full horse-freights; neither would they pay from 1858 to 1862; neither have they paid in 1872, as against horses.

A large part of the boats own and carry their horses, two teams (four horses), alternating the teams from boat to tow-path every six hours. Many desire to see the hardships, cruelties and dangers to horses obviated. It is said that one company during the war, when most of the best drivers turned soldiers, lost as many horses during the season as they put on for all their boats in the spring; that is, they had to purchase a complete equipment to make good their losses.

Some humane captains tow by the "lines" to avoid suffering and dangers to horses, many of which are drowned, and many left by the wayside. When changed from tow-path to stable, a stout man must hold the horse by the tail as he descends the steps into the stable, to prevent his pitching against the opposite side; and he holds with greater difficulty as he descends the bridge from the high, light boat to the tow-path, which is often more dangerous than the stable descent.

Others tow by the "lines"—take turns for teams, often with tedious delays—and they are, to a great extent, *subservient to the drivers*, else they suffer by their indifference, laziness or caprices, and many are sure to do their "poorest," unless they are feed extra.

All would be charmed with towage by steam, if done with economy, dispatch, regularity and safety; but quite another feeling prevails under the suggestions of changing drivers for engineers, stables for engine-rooms, horses for machinery, and light cargos for full ones, as in case of converting the horse-boat to a steamer.

Steam, as used for towing purposes, would be acceptable and subservient to the several thousand boatmen constantly in service.

If we give to the automaton system of steam *any privileges* over horse-boats—excepting for incidental initiatory encouragement to steam—we have a war of the many against the few. In the former era the double toll system was obliged to be suspended, and the no-toll system of this era is only a temporary sufferance.

Therefore, steam must stand or fall by its own merits, and should be fostered and developed until horses possess no competitive ability.

Canal Necessities.

The history of the experiments for means of propulsion on our canals shows that no system has been developed by means of which the carrying power of these great channels of communication can be made available by steam. If this deplorable fact is to be overcome, it must be through the aid of the inventor; we must have some instruments of propulsion not hitherto in use, and some other means of application of the propelling power than those now in practice, or steam can never be sufficiently utilized to supersede horses on canals.

We see the New York and Albany tow-boats, with from twenty to forty loaded canal boats, running at four miles per hour, and they have taken over sixty boats in a single tow from New York to Albany. But an engine, with a respectable part of their steam, can take but a *small fraction* of their boats, and at a largely reduced speed on the canal.

The doom of 1845, of 1858 to '62, and of 1871 to '72, hangs over steam like a shroud; it is a mechanical doom. Steam should be mechanically elevated so that it can utilize from a third to half of its power, and so that an engine can develop an equivalent of thirty to fifty horses on the tow-path to a train of boats, and so that it can take trains of ten to fifteen boats on the two sixty-miles levels—where large hulls can be built and used without necessity of passing locks—and somewhat smaller trains on the other parts of the canal, averaging eight to ten boats per tug, or moving from 70,000 to 80,000 bushels of corn, all as fast as they can be safely handled, and then the day of horses is limited, and canals will need new arrangements, new regulations and new customs.

Tugs on the canal have never exceeded a utility of eight to fifteen per cent. of the inherent power of their steam. Hence, they have never had towing power to develop the movement of trains of boats; but when they can be made mechanically to utilize from thirty to fifty per cent., the train movement becomes initiated with boats just as absolutely as with cars, and the tow-boat system will be just as prominently and universally established between Buffalo and Albany as it is between New York and Albany.

It is perfectly practical for steam, when it shall possess a respectable mechanical adaptation to canal duty; that is, when it shall not be so shamefully profligate in expenditures of power—*to double the average speed of horses, or lessen the general average of ten days on the canal to five days*, of which the down trips may overrun and the up trips fall short, as with horse average.

When a single tug shall equal 30 to 50 horses on the tow-path, it equals 60 to 100 of supply, as all require the alternate team.

The automaton system of steam is a hinderance to horse-boat navigation, besides increasing the risks and dangers, whilst the towing system, in substitution for horses, greatly improves the navigation and lessens the risks and dangers. Averaging the total mileage of a season with horse-boat times of transit, and boats meet each other every twenty minutes, night and day including Sundays, for seven months. To carry this tonnage, there must be eleven meetings of steamers to nine by horses, which increases the risks and dangers twenty-two per cent.; on the other hand, tows to the same tonnage would only meet each other about every three hours, hence for long distances they have an unobstructed water way.

MECHANICAL INVENTION, to adapt steam to the heavy resistances of canal boats, is therefore the first and greatest necessity of canals.

A second necessity will be AUXILIARY AND CO-OPERATIVE POWER AT THE LOCKS AND SHORT LEVELS.

These must be local, and may be by stationary steam-power, by water-power from the upper levels, or by horses.

Thus, there would be only one detention of a tug through

all the sixteen locks from West Troy to Cohoes—only one wherever there are two or more locks near each other, and at all locks there must be an independent local power to handle all boats. In this way tugs will lose less time between Buffalo and Albany than horse-boats do in changing teams from boat to tow-path every six hours.

Following these necessities, new rules, regulations and customs will be established, protecting the rights and equities of all.

A third necessity will be a CENTRALIZED MANAGEMENT, or control of all tugs, train-movements, and local powers at short levels and locks.

This is essential to a harmony of movements, to a proper distribution of motors, and to a proper adaptation to all the ebbs and flows of trade. This is just as essential for the tugs of a canal as for the locomotives of a railway. Provided the control of steam shall be held, *upon the merits of some invention*, protected by Letters Patent from the General Government; then the owners thereof might establish a centralized management to meet the merits, demands and exigencies of the case. They could enforce a harmony of interests between all trains and a harmony of police regulations, and they could enfore a consolidation of effort and co-operation to meet any exigency, just as a railway company can consolidate and develop its efforts upon any necessitous occasion.

In the nature of the case, these three necessities, when accomplished, will give to steam *the universal movement of boats.*

First.—Because it becomes a cheap motor in regard to which horses can hold no competitive claim.

This is seen from the fact that when steam can only utilize from eight to twelve per cent. of its power, as under the two eras of steam, the two best steamers—the *S. B. Ruggles* and *City of Buffalo*—lived five years in competition with horses, nothing since has exceeded their economies or capabilities; but give the steam they used a utility of thirty to fifty per cent., or over three times its present capabilities, and no team can be supported in competition.

Second.—Because it possesses the economies of concentrated power.

Horse-power must be diffused into small and limited qualities to be economical. The cost of double, treble, or quadruple teams, to increase speed or reduce time, swells the cost of transportation almost in like ratio, and would eat largely into the value of cargoes.

With the *present enormous waste of steam-power, trains with over three boats* begin to increase the cost of freight per ton. The *Governor King* was less economical with five boats than with three. On a part of the Eastern Division, two powerful tugs, lashed side by side on the levels, have taken a train of (17) seventeen boats successfully. Give to half their combined steam fifty per cent. addition to their combined power, and train movement receives an important inauguration. Economy, dispatch, regularity and a universal harmony of interests prevail.

SUMMARY.

The considerations of facts and suggestions herewith presented, embody important reasons for the Legislature to continue in force the Act of April, 1871, "to foster and develop the inland commerce of the State." It seems well adapted to influence, encourage and facilitate the development of mechanical, inventive talent; and to this end, all interests pertaining to the immediate elevation of canals, to the benefits of steam, should co-operate.

To encourage invention to utilize the steam is of paramount importance, because the other "*necessities*" will then be met, and they need no legislation, for common business talent will supply their demands.

The MECHANICAL NECESSITIES of our canals are greater than pertain to any possibilities by the old systems of propulsion. *It is not sufficient for steam to barely or doubtfully compete with horses, it should supersede them with the same superiorites and same universality* that it has on railways.

Where steam is mechanically adapted to its uses, horses bear no comparison to its economies ; hence, give steam its required mechanical adaptation to canals, and horses must be adandoned.

The enthusiasm of 1872, in regard to steam, is less than in 1858, but there is a deep feeling of necessity for steam permeating the community, and it should be encouraged and directed in the proper channel, for the anxieties of 1858 *foundered on incompetent mechanism*, and the anxieties of 1872 *are in the same impassable channel.*

The Governor's Message of 1873 renews the scheme which was prominently before the Legislature a few years since, which was to lengthen one tier of locks by gates of different construction, and so as to receive longer boats of present width ; yet a single thought will show that *this will not help steam ;* for the insatiable desire for maximum cargo will put the *Bull Head* boat into the long locks, just as it has into the present locks, and sharp steamers cannot compete with it.

It is proper to observe that such lengthening of *one tier* will first: coerce present boatman to sacrifice their property, which with boats and equipments, exceeds a valuation of twenty million dollars, or else cut the boats into two parts, and lengthen them (and strengthen their sides and "back-bones") to the full capabilities of the lengthened locks ; for the short boats cannot compete with the long ones.

Then, when the mass are altered, they will coerce the State to alter the second tier, because it becomes worthless and inoperative, and because the one tier becomes incapable of passing so great a multitude of boats, and it would otherwise greatly reduce the carrying capacity of the canals.

The State is sure to complete the removal of the "benches" on the remaining part of the "Eastern Division" as they are already removed from a part, and from the Middle and Western Division ; and then we can find no fault with the canal. *But this will not help steam* vs. *horses.* All improvements help horses equally with steam, and there is the ever-pending difference of cargo.

The same authority discusses the advantages to follow, "if

the time can be shortened from Buffalo to New York from (14) fourteen to (5) five days," &c. If a hundred thousand dollars reward *for expedition*, pending during two seasons of navigation, has proved insufficient to reduce the *average* of the three shortest trips with, 200 tons cargo, below seven days total or actual time from Buffalo to West Troy, the five days to New York, with the present knowledge of steam machinery, becomes an impossibility. But newspapers have preceded the message with the false supposition and the same error.

The extraordinary measures initiated by the N. Y. Central R. R., by their forty million dollars issue of bonds for the construction of *a double track exclusively for freight*, shows the growing importance of this already immense business, and whilst automaton steamers, *under the known mechanism of the age*, will inevitably lessen the carrying capacity of the canal, by filling its locks—which alone control the maximum carrying capacity—eleven times with light cargoes in place of nine times with full freights; *the mechanical elevation* and substitution of steam, as shown by the CANAL NECESSITIES herein set forth, possesses still more extraordinary importance.

Every consideration enforces the NECESSITIES, set forth in this appeal, OF MECHANICAL IMPROVEMENT, LOCAL AUXILIARY POWER, AND CONCENTRATED MANAGEMENT.

www.ingramcontent.com/pod-product-compliance
Lightning Source LLC
LaVergne TN
LVHW011141110826
845150LV00008B/2446

9781418193515